For Ch

Micheal O'Siadhail

February 5th 2024

"These timely poems capture the multiple challenges of our times with keen insight and lively passion. O'Siadhail's vision is a haunting plea to awaken to compassionate realignment with the living Earth community. His skillful entanglement of grave urgency and creative hope makes this compelling—indeed, required—reading."

—**MARY EVELYN TUCKER**, co-director of the Yale Forum on Religion and Ecology and co-author of *Journey of the Universe*

"In *Desire*, Micheal O'Siadhail presents us with four epic poems that are stunning in their sweep. With his keen eye for detail, O'Siadhail paints a vivid portrait of humanity reminiscent of Dante's circles of hell. Like a modern day Jeremiah, this poet with the voice of a prophet rails against the greed, self-indulgence, and carelessness that threaten life on Earth. In so doing, the tapestry he weaves incorporates economics, politics, big business, instant gratification, social media, privacy, depletion of resources, climate change, democracy, and capitalism. The poems are comprehensive, exhaustive, and completely relevant in their contemporary-ness. Yet, they are grounded in history and anchored in biblical references. O'Siadhail gleans deep lessons from the pandemic that hovers over all four poems. And in the end, he uplifts us with the redemptive love of his God."

—**GEORGETTE F. BENNETT**, founder and president of the Tanenbaum Center for Interreligious Understanding and co-author of *Religicide: Confronting the Roots of Anti-religious Violence*

"O'Siadhail poses one of the most pressing questions of our day: 'Have we learnt what matters most of all?' He sets it in the broad sweep of a poetic diagnosis of the climate crisis, global pandemic, misinformation, and surveillance capitalism and challenges us to consider what forms of desire would honor the goodness and givenness and limits of our common home."

—**MIROSLAV VOLF, MATTHEW CROASMUN, AND RYAN McANNALLY-LINZ**, authors of *Life Worth Living*

"In this superb collection, Micheal O'Siadhail once again sees poetry as a revelatory form of knowledge which offers otherwise unavailable insights into the world in which we live. He connects Covid-19, the destruction of the planet, and capitalism in the digital age, and looks at desire across these intersectional contexts. He sees the desire for success and power as culpable, but also envisages desire as a positive way through the current morass to a better political, social and ethical world: 'What desire will shape a world we're left?' As is typical of O'Siadhail, this is achieved through a dazzling array of rhyme schemes and evocative language."

—**EUGENE O'BRIEN**, Professor of English Literature and Theory at Mary Immaculate College and director of the MIC Institute for Irish Studies at the University of Limerick

"Micheal O'Siadhail's new cycle of poems, *Desire*, is a soaring mythic reflection on our time. The great poet's wisdom, humor, compassion, and razor-wire sensibilities explore the fate of our new century as we ricochet between hope and hopelessness. The world is ready and waiting for this poetry. Yearning for it, really."

—**SHOSHANA ZUBOFF**, author of *The Age of Surveillance Capitalism* and Professor Emeritus, Harvard University

Desire

Micheal O'Siadhail

BAYLOR UNIVERSITY PRESS

© 2023 by Baylor University Press
Waco, Texas 76798

All Rights Reserved. No part of this publication may be reproduced,
stored in a retrieval system, or transmitted, in any form or by any means,
electronic, mechanical, photocopying, recording, or otherwise, without the
prior permission in writing of Baylor University Press.

Cover and book design by Elyxandra Encarnación
Cover art: Hofmann, Hans (1880–1966), *Rising Moon*, 1965, © ARS, NY.
With permission of the Renate, Hans & Maria Hofmann Trust / Artists
Rights Society (ARS), New York. Photo by Art Resource, NY.

Library of Congress Cataloging-in-Publication Data

Names: O'Siadhail, Micheal, 1947- author.
Title: Desire / Micheal O'Siadhail.
Description: Waco, Texas : Baylor University Press, 2023. | Summary:
  "Poetic reflections on contemporary crises and challenges such as
  climate change, COVID-19, digital capitalism, and consumerism"--
  Provided by publisher.
Identifiers: LCCN 2023025948 (print) | LCCN 2023025949 (ebook) |
  ISBN 9781481320061 (hardcover) | ISBN 9781481320092 (adobe pdf) |
  ISBN 9781481320085 (epub)
Subjects: LCGFT: Poetry.
Classification: LCC PR6065.S54 D47 2023 (print) | LCC PR6065.S54
  (ebook) | DDC 821/.914--dc23/eng/20230814
LC record available at https://lccn.loc.gov/2023025948
LC ebook record available at https://lccn.loc.gov/2023025949

Printed in the United States of America on acid-free paper with a
minimum of thirty percent recycled content.

For Christina and David

Contents

Acknowledgments

Thanks are due to *The Irish Times* and to *Commonweal*, where poems were first published.

Foreword

In *The Five Quintets*, in conversation with some of the main movers and shakers throughout the four hundred or so years of modernity, I attempted to move towards a vision for the twenty-first century.[1]

It was a long, slow process: ten years of reading, thinking, conversing, and writing, distilling as well as I could, into poetry in a variety of forms, a wisdom drawn from many fields—literature and the arts, economics, politics, the sciences, philosophy and theology—in order to offer orientations for life now. It resulted in some core insights into the truths, values, practices, and guiding figures that we most needed as our world entered what felt like a new, uncertain period. *The Five Quintets* was published in 2018. It wrestled not only with the complex, global legacy of Western modernity, but also with the aftermath of signal events of the early twenty-first

---

[1]   David Ford, "Seeking a Wiser Worldview in the Twenty-First Century: Micheal O'Siadhail's *The Five Quintets*", parts I and II, *Studies: An Irish Quarterly Review* 437 and 438 (2021): 59–83, 213–30.

century that had already shaken our world, such as 9/11 in the US and the 2008–2009 global financial crisis.

I was already at work following up *The Five Quintets* in relevant areas such as the environmental crisis. Then came the stupendous surprise of the global Covid-19 pandemic. Suddenly, all the previous, slowly accumulated insights and orientations were being stress-tested, and every country in the world was facing extreme challenges on many fronts. Life felt newly vulnerable and uncontrollable, interwoven and precious. Themes of *The Five Quintets*, such as seeking justice with generosity and compassion for all, humility in the face of our complex, unpredictable reality, the significance of the sciences, and the need to sound the depths of meaning in each of our traditions seemed freshly relevant, but they also cried out for new expressions and applications.

The world was facing a critical decade to which the themes of *The Five Quintets* are both relevant and in need of new improvisation.

In early spring of 2020, as the Covid-19 pandemic was spreading across the world, it was a time of great fear, a time like no other since the influenza of 1918. It is so extraordinary, in such an era of sophisticated technology and medicine, that a virus, a parasitic pathogen, could bring our world to its knees! Lockdown, the prison term for when prisoners are confined to their cells following a disturbance, entered our common parlance.

The lockdown disrupted our norms, and the enforced retreat allowed us to reflect on our lifestyles, to question our purposes, to take a broader view of our culture and our place in the world. Why such an increase in deadly viruses? Why are we so frantically seeking success? What is worth devoting our lives to? The more I thought about this time of the Coronavirus, the more it bore in on me that it was a crisis inextricably and complexly interlinked with the other two major, looming crises which had previously absorbed me—the destruction of the planet and rampant capitalism of the digital age.

Clearly, the pandemics that have occurred with greater frequency are bound up with climate change and the abuse of the environment. There are multiple connections. Many experts now believe that human behaviour that accelerates climate change and ignores biodiversity is the root cause of such pandemics. Both global warming and deforestation bring us in contact with new pathogens. The source of diseases is often wild animals, previously inhabiting environments where there were no humans, who are hunted for exotic foods. SARS, for example, is understood to have come from the connection between bats, carnivores and unsuspecting humans. Or think of how we fly all over, trailing pollution behind us, and how Covid-19, hitching a lift, raged across the globe. Given that pandemics may be closely linked to how we are destroying our planet, I felt that any meditation on the main dilemmas of our times had to face the dangers to our habitat.

Similarly, the exploitations of the high-tech companies are intertwined with the pandemic and with the environmental crisis. In July 2020, Elizabeth Farries of the Irish Council for Civil Liberties reported that there was concern in Ireland that an app intended to facilitate contact tracing to prevent the spread of Covid-19 might be neither "effective nor rights-respecting".[2] Those concerned with civil liberties were conscious of the dangers of data harvesting. Our physical environment has been threatened since the onset of the Industrial Revolution. Perhaps now there is also a psychological menace which drives environment-damaging consumerism and is the source of inordinate wealth and power for a few. About this time, I read Shoshana Zuboff's extraordinary book, *The Age of Surveillance Capitalism*,[3] which illustrates how the conveniences of the technological revolution which my generation has experienced can also be ominous instruments of control and power which spur behaviours so detrimental to our humanity and to the earth. The high-tech giants, providing us with sorely needed means of communicating and doing business during phases of lockdown, have greatly increased their wealth because of the pandemic.

The destruction of our environment, with all its dire consequences, and invidious surveillance conducted by the high-tech companies are both largely driven by greed. Often, what started with noble motives descended into a crude rapacity controlled by the high priests of computer skills. It seems to me that such avarice, this bottomless craving for wealth and power, is a strange perversion of healthy human desire. In the light of all that people have suffered during this pandemic, any reassessment of our values, any pondering of our age must ask: what is worthy of our desire? The ultimate question in our frail and passing human lives must be: what do we desire?

---

[2]   Elizabeth Farries, "Covid-Tracing App May Be Ineffective and Invasive of Privacy", *The Irish Times*, Tuesday, May 5, 2020.
[3]   Shoshana Zuboff, *The Age of Surveillance Capitalism* (New York: Hachette Book Group, 2019).

There is, of course, a hierarchy of desire. In an attention economy, digital capitalism deliberately seeks to dominate our attention to satisfy immediate desires. In a culture of distraction, how can we find the time to ask the bigger questions about meaning and what rightly attracts our energy and our talents? How can we ever have the serenity to sense the coherence of all life, to trust the abundance of being, to catch a prayerful glimpse of the eternal? The instantaneous indulgence of whims and wishes leaves little opportunity to discern how best we serve creation and what merits our lifetime's pursuit.

Covid-19 has been a lesson in humility, in how we are not in complete control and how we are part and parcel of nature. In the urgent need to think communally, we are aware as never before how interwoven our world really is. In such a pandemic, mask-wearing and social distancing are both self-protection and compassionate consideration of others. Acts of excessive individualism and lack of accountability only hastened the spread of the virus.

Similarly, our threatened planet shows us how we are stewards, not masters, and how, for all our technology and apparent dominance, we remain keepers, not lords. The reaction of nature to our abuse and extraction respects no fixed borders or boundaries and, in complicated ways, is also a contributory cause to pandemics.

The new digital wave of capitalism, both in its surreptitious gathering of marketable information, and even more so in its neo-behaviourist endeavours to amass wealth and power, is another exercise of control which aims to direct our consumption. Our excessive consumerism, in turn, harms the earth. Here, as in the case of our environmental crisis, we must keep on adapting and refining laws that demand accountability and openness.

I come back to desires. In the end, it seems to me that the motivation to inspire a change in this coming pivotal decade will stem from a ranking of our desires. Will all our lesser desires be steered by an overriding desire to embrace openly and respectfully the richness and variety of our world and to care for all?

> Is there one outstanding moment when
> We find a peace in simply knowing how
> There's no need to find desires again?
> All our being wants us to avow
> One desire so full that there is now
> Nothing needed over and above
> Letting fame and fortune be to love.

Epigraph

A pest will pass, all will be said and done—
Yet in its wake will we be more aware
How nature's filigree is frail and one,
Where neighbours' keepers breathe one Gardener's air?

But have our garden's climate changes led
To wildlife shifts so we live cheek by jowl
With raging viruses we host and spread
Around this now endangered globe we foul?

We want and want more than a life requires—
The masters of the net who push their wares
Will grab and bend our minds with ghost desires.
No time for contemplation's garden prayers.

Beyond our avarice, our greed's stillbirth,
What's worth desiring now for all we're worth?

Pest

1

Globe-trotting pest, jet-setting parasite,
Nabbing victims everywhere the same,
Riding on a breath nowhere airtight—
Do we planet-spoilers bear the blame?
No enough, why seek a blame or cause
Or rehearse what our frail world went through?
Best living in what is than in what was,
Let the past just pass and start anew.
All such memories should we best discard—
Ships when ploughing on forget their wake—
Or for the dead and for tomorrow's sake
Seek to mend a globe our greed has marred?
Through remembrance we salute the dead;
Tragedies look back to look ahead.

2

Covid, we had named this enemy
That's aware how globally we mesh,
Knows we sweat in each Gethsemane,
Fear we'll go the way of all good flesh.
Why this need for such a common foe—
Virus showing its respect for none?
So easy to forget what we now know
How our frail humanity is one.
In death's shadow all intensified—
As this ends how will we reconcile
Life before and after and decide
In our frailty now what is worthwhile.
In the light of thousands now bereft,
What desire will shape a world we're left?

3

No, we do not own our mother sphere,
We, whose role is steward and leasee,
In our greed are still so cavalier
Sundering our own nature's filigree.
Climates shift and beings all migrate
Shunning warmer parts from which they've fled,
Changing how we creatures all relate,
Passing unknown viruses that spread.
Still so much that no one understands:
Will there be more waves? Will it mutate?
Staying far apart and washing hands,
We relearn forbearance and we wait.
Nature shimmies far beyond our ken,
Teaching us humility again.

One coronavirus—who'd have thought?
Needing to discover the unknown,
We become the lordly cosmonaut
Claiming all this cosmos as our own.
Fly-bys, probes that orbit and then land
Gearing up to walk on planet Mars;
Yet to come a spaceship landing manned—
Spacefaring human reaching for the stars.
We the once earthbound who walked the moon
Underrated viruses' impact;
In our achievements did we seem immune,
In our pride were we too slow to act?
By one virus brought back down to scale,
In our glory earthlings still so frail.

4

April just when half our globe would bloom,
Nature signals time to resurrect,
Fat Dutch hyacinths spread spring's perfume
And burgeonings decide to leaf unchecked.
World so beautiful and unaware
Covid sneaked around a planet's girth,
Played its hide-and-seek me anywhere,
Bringing our illusions down to earth.
Cities of unease so eerie now,
Locking down for fear by touch or breath
We'd infect each other, dreading how
So unknowingly we dealt in death.
Out of sight it chalked up its own score,
Questioning all lives we'd lived before.

Newscasters counted thousands worldwide dead.
What do thousands mean? Each death is one.
In each digit see one face instead,
Someone's father, mother, daughter, son.
Sleepless cities' newfound silent nights
In strange muteness tossed in their distress,
Woke to sirens, red-blue flashing lights
Hastening through a sombre noiselessness.
Fingered ones before they know confined
In seclusion pests could not outsmart—
All beloved faces left behind—
In last agonies were set apart.
Cared for by a kind but masked unknown,
Tended to the end, they died alone.

5

Cunning spy invading our airspace,
Undercover agent who'd access
All our need to touch and to embrace,
Catching us off guard in one caress.
Even in our talk it could begin
Hiding droplets in the spray of tongues,
In our words the enemy within
Bent on colonising others' lungs.
Clever virus spreading still lay low
Several days allowing us pass on
What we've had and didn't even know,
Making us its covert liaison.
Multiplying secretly in you,
Covid played its game of peekaboo.

Beds and gurneys crowded on each floor,
New field hospitals, posts heads assign;
Medicine embraced war's metaphor—
Doctors redeployed to the front line.
Each new shift, a last shift's patient dead,
Others in grave danger had arrived;
Homing time, too tired or too in dread
To revisit, see who has survived.
Breathless, suffocating multiply—
Ventilators scarce, how then to choose
Who to help and who they should let die,
Life you'd likely save or likely lose?
How to be, while hardened to the task,
One last caring face behind a mask?

6

Hospitals all coped and tried to plan
Hiring as the endless death tolls grow
Yet one more refrigerated van
To absorb their morgue's new overflow.
Wary of the spikes and curves they chart,
Half protecting others, half in dread,
Masked we sought to walk six feet apart,
Conscious of the toll of daily dead.
Separated, trying to be brave,
Still some tiny courtesies displayed,
Signs of solidarity, a wave—
Which of us deep down was not afraid?
Fear now stalked our globe's Gethsemane—
Father, may this chalice pass from me.

How we wonder might all this have been
If there was no web or cyberspace,
Just suppose we had not been by screen
Virtually conversing face to face.
Busy, all those friends with time we lose,
Who for years we'd always meant to call—
Time to spare, once more we would swap news.
Have we learnt what matters most of all,
How we're loved, what love in turn we give?
On a monitor old warmth re-found,
Bound anew so much we could relive,
Covering our forgotten common ground.
More together in enforced withdrawal,
Nettedness that bound us one and all.

7

Youth infects those older unaware—
Covid separated young and old,
Rites of passage we'd by nature share,
To survive we had to place on hold.
Even those whom pathogens bereave,
Fearing they might help the virus spread,
Could no longer congregate to grieve,
Dare not gather to lament their dead.
Weddings planned with lists of guests and gifts,
Fear of spread infection would upend,
Birth alone among our threshold shifts,
Dread of Covid-19 can't still suspend.
Overspill of being, rich and rife—
Covid couldn't curb this rite of life.

Many maskless athletes didn't care,
All those breathless joggers on their run
Spraying reckless sweat-beads through the air,
Sure that they would never be the one.
Foolhardiness of those still young or strong,
Sure it wasn't yet their turn to die;
Heedless they might kill if they were wrong
Both themselves and all who pass them by.
Cavalier, still carefree and unchecked
Some among the smitten had not shown
Signs of illness but could yet infect
Those who aged were in the danger zone.
Caution would have served for all our sakes;
Others may have died from such mistakes.

8

Some cocooned far off from death as yet—
Though aware the crisis was full-blown,
Even if no friend had died they'd get
Word of one that friends of friends had known.
As they made a call just checking in
They had found that friends had lost a friend
From their childhood, almost kith and kin,
Who was buried when none could attend.
Weeks before they'd shared an evening meal—
'Let's not wait so long next time', they'd said.
No one had imagined this ordeal,
Ten days from infection he was dead.
Closer then than plotted graphs or trends—
One remove, each face of friends of friends.

Disappointments, things postponed, chagrin,
Dreams so many had to then let go;
Know there was no point in living in
Past subjunctives 'if it weren't so.'
How quickly isolation turns to hell—
Troubled, wanting it to end we'd miss
Moments that we might have savoured well
Conjuring perfections after this.
In our seclusion was there also peace,
Carefreeness of undistracted days,
Liberation from sideshows, release,
Time for being grateful and to praise?
What was and what will be life won't allow —
Even in confinement our sweet now.

9

Highway signs were warning overhead
How to flatten the infection curve,
Signalling 'Stay Home and Stop the Spread',
Guidance we'd been learning to observe.
All who tracked the spread on our behalf
Told how isolation gave us hope;
Showing us at last a flattened graph,
They believed we'd see a downward slope.
Thoughtless, will we underestimate
How a pest waits in the long grass still,
Drop our guard, mistake a lesser rate
For a charted line that dips to nil?
God knows what lives hinged on how we'd behave—
Letting up we'd tempt a second wave.

Many now fret tortured by unease,
Fearful how in time they'd make ends meet,
Households cooped with every cough and sneeze,
Others on their own in this retreat.
When so many suffer was it wrong
That some greeted light with thankfulness,
Were as grateful as the day was long?
Everything they have they loved to bless.
In confinement they had all they want:
Food and shelter in well-sunlit rooms,
With their lover, spouse or confidante,
All content until the world resumes.
Thankful they were not locked down alone,
Some could thrive in love's eternal zone.

10

Washing hands again and over again
Our new ritual throughout the day,
Soaping off each traitor pathogen,
Some would sing while others chose to pray
Long enough for 'Happy Birthday' twice.
Bored with happy birthdays someone said,
Certain that his timing was precise,
Better two *Our Fathers* prayed instead.
Finger-twining foam and froth and rub,
Knuckles, joints and wrists with so much care,
Sudsy palms our bubbling nail tops scrub—
How to love this sensuous affair!
Second time around *thy kingdom come*—
Patiently to swirl each lathered thumb.

Newscasts told how more have been laid off
Than amid the crash of twenty-nine;
Fear of such an economic trough
Now became our politics' fault line.
Cool economists would stake their claim,
How much loss can any state withstand?
Pressure rose, reopening became
Cabin-fevered citizens' demand.
Medical advisers resolute
Kept to counselling more tests, more swabs,
Asked if business eager to reboot
Forced a choice between lives lost and jobs?
Even as we thought we passed the peak,
We're as strong as we uphold the weak.

11

Sunday and our latitude warmed May;
Months from when this turmoil had begun
We unbent to recreate, to play,
Celebrate this day still named for sun.
Easily we were tempted to forget,
Set aside anxiety and fears;
Warmed, take off our masks, ignore the threat
And catch up with our pleasures in arrears.
Sun seduced us but we could resist—
In our warmth we should remain aware;
Danger still was roaming in our midst,
We were walking in the same nightmare.
Seeking, finding, sneaking, busy pest,
Covid knew no sabbath, knew no rest.

Hard to fight when you don't understand
By what dangers you are still beset;
It might still undo rebounds we'd planned.
Know your enemy—we didn't yet.
'Test and track', the cry was our attempt
To contain this pest. Should we rely
On declaring all come through exempt
Still unsure once bitten meant twice shy?
We were hanging hopes on some vaccine,
Even though we knew it might change tack,
By just subtly altering a gene,
Playing hide and seek make its comeback.
Enemies retreat to best return;
We had no choice, we had to wait to learn.

12

Once the Black Death threatened humankind;
'Bless you!' we respond still to a sneeze—
Thought to be its start, and to remind
Us how we're still prey to new disease.
Plagues we've only read of turn so real,
Every pest reverbing from the past
As we watched coronavirus steal
All across our shrunken globe so fast.
We just said 'be well!', 'be safe!', 'take care!'—
Owning up to just how frail we're still;
Though bless is not a word all moderns dare,
Nothing changes in our love's goodwill.
May each blessing anyhow expressed,
Hallow all who die from every pest.

Worldwide citizens would now begin
Stopping in a street or anywhere
To applaud and raise a goodly din,
Clapping up a thankfulness all share.
For all tenders our one grateful sign,
Those who lived from shift to shift in fear,
Medics, nurses holding our front line,
Often lacking sealed protective gear.
Now it's reckoned at the very least
One in ten infected as they worked;
Still unknown how many since deceased—
No one could have blamed them if they shirked.
Scattered noise could lift a city's mood;
Strange commotion of our gratitude.

13

So few cars on any city street
Pigeons left their nests and swirled between
Highrise ledges, fearless land to eat
Any mid-street grain or scrap they'd glean.
Told to stay home most acquiesce.
We then learn how unbeknownst we'd spare
All our cities and emitted less
Long-lived greenhouse gases in the air,
In New York or London, Paris, Rome
As our frenzied whirl restarts, when pressed
To create more jobs and we leave home,
Would we foul then worse our global nest?
Covid fear improved our habitat—
Nature's own backhanded caveat.

Long and winding buses seemed to glide
Empty through each spectral city's day,
Each on time though no one dared to ride—
Fearing closeness all had shied away.
Covid likes those surfaces that gleam,
All their seats and rails of steel or chrome;
Void, these shining corridors could seem
Like the 'deaf coach' spoken of back home.
Country people used to once believe
If you saw a silent coach you knew
This meant death, as it would only leave
Taking someone who belonged to you.
Covid, sending out its ghostly fleets
Drove deaf coaches through our cities' streets.

14

A disaster many lands would share—
How in nursing homes the cared-for died;
Awful paradox to be in care
When that care meant cases multiplied.
Tests began to show infected were
Residents and carers half and half;
One on one the spread could then occur,
Passed unwittingly by their own staff.
Knowing what we know we understand
Care could never hold the pest at bay;
All the closeness of each tending hand
Had they only known to keep away.
Death's embrace by those still good at heart—
Irony of care by care apart.

Lungs inflamed that fill, an organ fails,
Still so little known how it behaves;
No one yet was sure what it entails—
Was its guile now plotting further waves?
Redeployed outside their expertise,
Overwhelmed, uncertain of their tasks,
Doctors baffled by this sly disease,
Still conferred through muffled shields and masks.
Twelve-hour shifts they worked in crisis squads,
Tired and frightened, learning on the hoof;
Driven to seek cures against the odds,
This or that they'd try though with no proof.
Death the threat their schooling would defy—
Yet distraught they watched as roomfuls die.

15

Headlines, bulletins, the last news flash,
Updated all the figures, next death toll,
Forecasts of an economic crash—
Where's the world we thought we could control?
Knowing we were shaken to the core.
What old habits should we learn to shed?
Lives can't be as they had been before,
Speculation on what lay ahead.
Warned about our keeping safe, advice
How to cope with life in quarantine,
Everything but this was placed on ice,
Anything that's less might seem obscene.
Other themes discussed, however well,
Given this disease, a bagatelle.

Hard enough for youth when life's secure
To conceive what path they'll choose to tread;
Worse when elders were no longer sure
How the world would change in years ahead.
Fledglings so weighed down by all at stake,
Shouldn't at this time have had to care;
Asked to curb their youth for all our sake,
Some of whom so easily would despair.
Knowing or half-knowing they both are
Less in danger yet not fully safe;
Segregated in those months' bell jar,
Pent up energy would fret and chafe.
How could those who just had reached their prime,
Find their feet in such a stumbling time?

16

How the pest could catch us unaware—
Closeness was its ground for sabotage;
Shut each service for our body's care,
Hairdressing, spas or parlours for massage.
Hid behind each city's loud façade
Those forlorn, the lonely, the alone,
Citizens so often all too glad
For whatever tenderness they're shown
Or the chance to tell a groomer how
All had been since last time they had met,
Worries they confess, a quiet powwow,
Things unburdened through this soft outlet.
Covid threatened each consoling touch,
Loneliness's final straw to clutch.

'Round the globe same image on the news:
Outside storefronts people feet apart;
More like no-goods loitering than queues,
Lining up to take a shopping cart.
Learning new and strange standoffishness,
Stores had painted X's on the place
Where we stand in order to progress,
Moving on in turn from base to base.
Masked, we eyed each other yards away,
Nearly greeting almost to show proof
This is duty-done or just to say
It's not you that makes me seem aloof.
Smiles more from the eye than from the lip,
Kept our strange new distant fellowship.

17

News among concerned physicians breaks—
Covid had now found a slyer path;
What a stealthy turn this virus takes,
Catching children in its aftermath.
Somewhat like an aftershock we find
Medicos discover children can
Still contract disease which was defined
First by Kawasaki in Japan.
Infants but since Covid youngsters too
Rash, ablaze with fever, aches inside,
Arteries inflamed and then a few
Cases where the victim children died.
In its wake these lives it still can thieve,
Pests had new tricks up their deadly sleeve.

Experts talk of herd immunity
As all hastened still to test and screen;
It would take so long to guarantee
That four-fifths can get the right vaccine.
Sixteen thousand plus now volunteer
For experiments and out of these
Half would take new drugs they'd pioneer—
Though they'd all death-dice with this disease.
Young, still brimming with their lives ahead,
Gambling their own being so we could
Sidestep animals, and they instead
Serve to vaccinate for all our good.
Loving life each free-willed vaccinee
Dared preempt our herd humanity.

18

Snow although it was already May.
What explains such topsy-turvyness?
Is our habitat in disarray?
Mother Earth we've caused you such distress.
How will life for children's children be?
Could it be too late now to repair
Damage we have done and so should we
Fall into the black hole of despair?
Spare us from our smug despondencies.
Why do we demand our pride's quick fix?
We will best fight back from this disease
When reality and hope both mix.
Such despair a know-all arrogance,
Closing off the heart to change and chance.

Though at last it seemed we'd curbed the spread
As we warmed into May's final days;
They're three-fifty thousand worldwide dead,
Still some soothsaid yet another phase.
Death in any numbers is obscene—
Frontline doctors would in turn admit,
Overwrought and scarred from all they'd seen
Rather than face this again they'd quit.
Ventilated, an hour eight tenders stayed
Just to get a single patient turned;
Life and death decisions each shift made,
Left them each bewildered, strained, outburned.
Drained by all the lives they could not save,
Few could then endure a second wave.

19

Most had never datebooks blank before,
April and now May all vacant space,
Lined up days and dates and nothing more—
Strange how these months seemed a kind of grace.
Though before we'd filled in things to do
We enjoyed new stillness of recall,
Days to recollect and to review
Images in reverie we'd trawl.
Years we'd wanted to replay our life,
Summon up all friends alive and dead;
Now we came to understand Lot's wife,
Glancing back while Lot just looked ahead.
Peaceful empty-paged and waiting June,
Gentle time in memory's cocoon.

Outside all the dangers of the pest,
Unfamiliar world of mask and glove;
Inside then how could we be more blessed
Than to be cooped up with one we love?
In confinement we were now so free:
Days à deux and simple meals prepared,
Household chores divided as needs be;
Dovetailed rhythms of a dream that's shared.
Sad how for some pairs who stayed at home,
Lockdown would become a testing ground
Showing rifts of empty-nest syndrome,
Chasms unseen while others were around.
Dramas acted out behind closed doors,
Living hell or honeymoon encores.

20

Pests can tell us who our leaders are—
Probing, testing, trying for what's weak;
Choosing well we're guided by their star,
Choosing ill we're dazed by doublespeak.
Some walked well their leadership tightrope,
Heeding every argument and fact,
Hearten all by blending truth and hope,
Though aware of danger still could act.
Sadly the unfit were soon found out—
Those who blamed the rivals whom they smeared,
While they dithered or just faced about,
Showed how they cared most how they appeared.
Crises left failed leaders no excuse;
Fates of millions hang on those we choose.

Being home for some had seemed to shirk—
Habits from those years careers were built,
Old routines demanding always work;
Leisure though enjoyed still tinged with guilt.
Slower rhythms of such unrushed meals,
Chance to do those things so long dreamed of;
Listening and relearning how it feels
To enjoy long days with those they love.
Some who'd thought such joys beyond their ken
Ask what in God's name they'd striven for—
Not in need, and loath to start again,
Thought now that working less they might live more —
Gifts their drivenness could not foresee,
Time enough to live, to love, to be.

21

When our mobile telephones forecast
Warmth with highs of sixty-one degrees—
We thought we'd wake from this nightmare at last,
Find our sleep imagined this disease.
Warmth might make us so undisciplined,
We'd unmask, allow our face the sun,
Just to throw all caution to the wind,
Hug our friends as we had always done.
But not yet. Dread kept us on our toes.
We who still in thanks could walk God's earth,
Kept small disciplines we'd juxtapose
With enjoying sun for all we're worth.
Slung between angst's constant push and pull,
Fear's *qui vive* yet life lived to the full.

Slowly as the deaths then taper off,
Graphs of new infections flatten out,
Though new peaks may follow on this trough,
Yet already some began to doubt,
Wondered if they'd lost autonomy,
If they'd been for too long now hemmed in.
Medics do not grasp economy—
Time to let our old world rebegin.
Echoes of what Moses must have heard,
All those mumbled protests that he faced,
When again his people doubt his word—
Were they led from Egypt to this waste?
Greed for newer needs ignoring debts,
Short-term gratitude so soon forgets.

22

As this passed how would the future be?
Vaccinated could we plan and plot?
Still confined we dreamt of being free,
Free from the unknown no matter what.
All we knew was nothing was now sure—
We imagined parts but not the whole,
Such half-knowing made us insecure,
When we do not trust, we want control.
Like the lilies of the field we may
Come to thrive in all that still unknown,
Take no care then for the coming day,
For tomorrow brings some troubles of its own.
All intents and purposes now must
In our unknown future learn to trust.

Those who hold economies in flight,
Grounded, watched their businesses collapse,
No next plane to catch, no end in sight,
Watched as time refuses to elapse.
Happiest when in the whirl of things—
Frisson of hard sells or deals at stake;
Busy spirits lost for lack of wings,
Lockdown worst for those who move and shake.
Timeless yet no business they could drum—
Sand clock where the sand just would not flow.
Pasts seemed long ago, would futures come—
Half the sand above and half below?
Grains of sand caught in an hourglass neck,
Time on hold, all commerce still in check.

23

As the rates of death and spread subside
Metrics of this crisis now cry foul,
Slews of those who're poor or weak had died—
Too close, too clustered, breathing cheek by jowl.
Crisis means a judgement still in Greek—
How will this one have deemed the way we live?
Less we trust, the more and more we seek,
Fear has made us more acquisitive.
Us and them of have and having not—
Insecure we've been afraid to share;
Caring, we'd untie the Gordian knot,
Dream what is a little less unfair.
Covid is the push that comes to shove,
Judging we outdo our fear with love.

Think of early pictures from the moon
With our earth first seen there from afar;
Did we not believe that sometime soon
We'd be one, aware how small we are?
Pests don't need a flag or document
And which land is great it doesn't care—
Only jointly can we now prevent
Outbreaks when it's purged from everywhere.
Will some countries now begin to claim
How it's others' fault they can condemn,
Finding any scapegoats we can blame—
World re-sundered into 'us and them'?
Only globally this battle's won—
Surely we are greatest when we're one.

24

No respect for rank on its rampage
A pandemic was it seems dead set
On reaching every race and class and age,
Reaping grimly everywhere and yet,
Boxed in tight, the danger amplified,
Covid turned on those who're most in need;
Better off, some chose the countryside
Where less close the virus might not breed.
Innermost we know this is unfair—
Some could stay while others simply flee.
Nothing perfect, still we have to care—
We are each humanity's trustee—
All is not for nought if we have found
How things might be recast next time around.

Mothered by necessity we learn
How to meet consulting on the net;
Would our convection trails return,
Would we need again to flit and jet?
Global air improved research had found,
Nature's healing had by now begun
Only in the weeks we'd been earthbound—
Would this continue in the longer run?
Even months ago who would have thought
It could come about that everyone
Shunning flights as we had known we ought
Could undo the damage we have done?
Urgencies and wisdom coalesce,
Vision we have found in our distress.

25

Much that's damaged already we reclaim,
Still we wonder in the longer haul
Will our lives now ever be the same?
Surely twenty-twenty changed us all.
In our shells have we had time to think
Why such constant busyness and greed?
We can opt to pull back from the brink,
Learn to be content with what we need.
Will we choose to learn or to forget—
Business as before or watershed
Where we appropriate what's gained and let
Hindsight be our foresight's gift instead—
Knowing all we should before have known,
Twenty-twenty vision made our own.

Nature fired a shot across our bow;
But so former lives could rebegin.
Thanks to fevered scientists' knowhow,
We have reined one deadly virus in.
We say we care but yielding to our greed,
Never nail our colours to the mast;
Surely such a warning we should heed,
Not allow it fade into our past?
Mother Earth we think we can outsmart,
All the while we slide to ecocide;
Only changed desire can change our heart,
Cries the memory of all who died.
Letting how it is be how it was,
Covid we'll have curbed but not its cause.

Habitat

1

Garden given us to dress and keep
In our greed we mar;
Who on earth do we still think we are,
Dare we name ourselves as stewards now?
Dominance of all our idle boast—
Flights from ravaged habitats allow
Viruses to find their human host;
As we sow we reap.

Grieving God once bid for seven days
Noah built his ark,
Two by two earth's creatures would embark.
All things that swim or creep or crawl or fly,
Saving from that flood at most a pair.
In love's covenant they'd multiply;
Every being just in being there
Gives creation praise.

In our stewardship we can't forget
Heaven has begun,
Nature stewarded and we are one.
God who stayed the hand of Abraham
Shows creation love's self-sacrifice,
Lions may yet lie down beside a lamb;
Work in hand, unfolding paradise,
Now and still not yet.

2

What was once for all belonged to none,
Everyone was heir
To shared pasture or to everywhere
Food was grown. Have we forgotten how
Land is only ever ours on loan?
Do our walls and fences then allow
What was once for all become our own,
All belong to one?

Yet enclosures made for richer fields—
Single owners can
Vary what they need to grow and plan
In the light of all they've come to know
What maintains the soil's own opulence.
Year by year they alter what they sow,
Harvest in these larger fields they fence
Crops with ampler yields.

Commons walled and fenced, big farms succeed;
Those they dispossess,
Poor and now dependent, pastureless,
Leave to swell the cities. Soon we see
Reckless patterns in our blundering;
Progress driven by rapacity
Linking betterment to plundering
Shapes our dreams of greed.

3

Maybe from word go we've always been
Fouling our own nest,
Earth we humans gradually infest.
Romans trawl and overfish their seas,
Cities with their waste and stench pollute,
Easter Islanders had felled palm trees;
Since first Adam bit forbidden fruit,
Greed's selfish gene.

Hazy world of smog and soot we make,
Gases trapping heat;
Much we can't renew but still deplete.
Everything each restless whim consumes,
We mine, we frack, we fell, we slash and burn.
World of acid rain and carbon fumes,
Soon, too soon the point of no return—
All our earth at stake.

Nature's gifts we think are all our own,
Do not realise
All our need for more will jeopardise.
Ecocidal in our endless greed,
What of all that swim and fly and creep?
Crying out creation asks if we'd,
One with nature, learn to hold and keep
All not ours alone.

4

Once a worry in the longer run,
Somewhere years away
Our convenience's reckoning day;
Delicate complexes now defiled—
Heatwaves, raging fires and hurricanes,
Warmed-up globe where pests and plagues run wild,
Barely time enough to change remains—
Yet so little done.

Is a deal on such a global scale
Hopeless now to make?
Look what's managed when it's trade at stake!
We depend on fossil fuels, we plead,
Though we'd do with wind and water power.
Grit we lack? Still when in fiscal need
We've the will. At this eleventh hour
All excuses fail.

Yes, we know the danger but then why
Such half-heartedness?
Our free-marketeers won't acquiesce
Though all science urged us to reform—
World's zeitgeist mistimed by history
Saw us let our planet warm and warm.
Gone beyond all market sophistry,
Now we do or die.

5

In the market game it's win or fall,
Amplify or die—
We create demands we then supply.
Mother Earth's own storehouse running low,
Husbanding resources makes all sense.
Won't the markets let expansion go?
Still held back by our ambivalence,
All endeavours stall.

Even we who are convinced will tend,
Hedging every bet,
Not to push too hard at least as yet.
We don't stand our ground instead withdraw,
Once again don't dare to regulate,
Curb all corporate excess by law.
Will we leave what's needed far too late,
Fearing to offend?

If we hesitate a world's undone—
Here's our final chance,
Neither over-governed nor freelance
All as sibling keepers to combine
Newer working modes to tend the nest,
For each generation down the line
Let our mended biosphere attest
How on earth we're one.

6

Though we'd know or fathom how to deal
With such damage done
Or at least to limit one by one
Each ill usage of our habitat
Which still throws our globe in such a state,
Would we even dare to reckon that
Should we reform then at some future date
Planet earth might heal?

Will there be a change in who holds sway
So control returns
From big business to our own concerns?
Can we rise above the bottom line,
Reinterpret how to share our power
In such ways that let us redefine
How all lives are wound as one in our
Tangled interplay.

Deeper than all changes we might make
How we think must shift
And relearn it isn't in our gift
To expend creation to our will?
Thoughts reshape worldviews they underpin.
Even in our glory we are still
Humble stewards here embodied in
Nature's give and take.

7

Strange how knots of histories entwine—
Things occur we sought
That were near impossible we'd thought.
Can ecologists in time still urge
The improbable to come again?
Though so late to pull back from the verge,
Much may happen yet beyond our ken—
Even blue moons shine.

Slowly to persuade a world to care
And forego some ease,
Since we know we're now our heirs' trustees.
Even when proposals seem too vague
And in gloom we feel our way and grope,
All or nothing stances just renege—
Better tweak and tinker than lose hope,
Cop out in despair.

Such temptations to begin to doubt
Worth of what few do.
Going green, excesses they eschew
Seem faint candles in the dark they light,
While unsure what quivering flames achieve,
Wishful flickers in the satin night
That for all the darkness still believe
Nothing snuffs hope out.

8

Climate now the wind cone of this age
Wants us all to choose,
Side with one of two unlike worldviews.
We are questioned how we opt to live,
Forced in turn to home at counter-poles,
Openhanded or acquisitive;
Climate our barometer of souls,
Spirit pressure gauge.

Any curbs and some feel they're controlled —
Climate an excuse,
Yet another jealous scheme that skews
How the markets can forecast each need,
Easy ruse to pamper those who fail.
Commerce always driven by our greed,
Bigger means economies of scale;
What all have they hold.

Others see a crisis as rebirth.
Yes, we must survive—
Yet beyond duress how best to thrive?
Will the richer half come to agree
Who first fouled the nest first cleans?
Dare we think of global equity,
Weathering the threat become a means
To re-dream our earth?

9

Centuries we've been so profligate
Never had to care;
Slow and sure our reckless world aware
How all fossil fuels now menace us
Greenhousing us in dangerous climate swings.
Trusting science's cold calculus
We have learned unless we clip our wings
Soon it is too late.

Threatened oil tycoons searched out and found
Fakers to gainsay
All we're sure we learned and so delay
Curbing carbon spew by muddying
Waters we were sure were clear. Bemused,
Some to what we're used will choose to cling.
Oilmen want us stumbling and confused
On uncertain ground.

Books once cooked, their figures once massaged,
All that underlies
Faith in science as truth's enterprise
Compromised by lies for short-term gain
Sinks then into sands that shift and slide.
Hard to know how to believe again
What had been surefooted and worldwide.
Trust is sabotaged.

10

All the damage we have done and yet
Those who can't curtail
Meddling, would now on a global scale
Geoengineer to ease the heat—
Maybe block a segment of sun rays,
Or to fix a nature we can cheat,
Seas they'd plant to trap our carbon haze,
Playing earth roulette.

Given time there's nothing we won't know—
So we had believed—
Think of all technology achieved.
We'd main parts to nature's minor role,
Every threat could surely be foreclosed.
Some resent relinquishing control,
Hate the thought of discipline imposed,
Grudge their letting go.

If we'd had the courage to begin
Reining in our greed
When the world of scientists agreed
We're on course to ruin our habitat,
There would be less need to regulate.
So ironic how a technocrat
Who resists restraints, demands we wait,
Digs all deeper in.

11

We're aware our damage gathers pace,
Moves now near our own,
How Katrina's tropical cyclone
Maimed New Orleans, or how heatwaves
Scorch beyond what we had known before
And even so we're still convenience slaves
Who consume and somehow half-ignore
Signs of what we face.

Now by such and such a year they say
Four Celsius degrees
Warmer world and ice sheets will unfreeze,
Swathes of earth will flood or overheat.
Though our heads don't doubt all this is true—
Cataclysms too remote to meet,
Prophecies of dark we know we're due
Seem still far away.

Hard to heed what is less now than then—
While we don't deny
How disaster threatens us and why,
Busy in each day's own griefs and joys
Holding on for all we're worth to hope,
In the sweetness of our life's white noise
We remember how we need to cope,
Then forget again.

12

Shrewd developers' keen weather eye
Trusts each new ill wind
Will yet blow them good—their greed is pinned
On ruined land where villages have been.
Smart insurers too by subterfuge
Hike their bottom line; well-off begin
Building seawalls, fearing no deluge
They'll be high and dry.

Politicians yet too hand-in-glove
With the business game
Know for cutbacks they would take the blame,
How few voters ever think ahead.
Playing safe still most prevaricate,
Shelve what must be done and have not led—
Limits all too little, all too late
Given from above.

Long-spooned folk who with the devil sup
Will not now succeed
Only in the end when they must heed
Widespread calls for change will they then act,
As when mass demands claim civil rights
For life's victims though the odds are stacked
Years against them till a world unites
From the bottom up.

13

Almost like a debt of smog and grime
We're now paying for,
So we think this built up long before
Our own time when industry began.
Yet the half of all that we have ruined
Happened in one three-decade's brief span,
Mother earth sustaining half her wound
During one lifetime.

What a restless species we now are
Hurtling here and there,
Jetting fuel vapour through the air,
Gadding on our motorways non-stop.
Spoilt first world uneasy in our core,
We still drive and fly and country-hop
Smirching as we never had before,
Roam this earth we mar.

Deadly virus stowaways conspire,
Find their hosts worldwide,
On our unrest spongers hitch a ride.
Could we not explore here where we are—
Wonder and the ordinary merge—
Ask ourselves why should we journey far
Or what drives disquiet's consuming urge?
What do we desire?

14

Commons now turned land one can possess—
This, because it's said,
Overused all common land is bled,
So resources are best owned by one;
To succeed each one succeeds alone,
Which means that some have lost while those who've won
Sit then pretty owning all they own—
World's self-centeredness.

Poor and tired the huddled masses teem.
Breathing free they trust
New world's dream of endless golden dust—
If not for me, at least offspring of mine.
Wealth no matter what turns greed's black hole,
Sweated labour's mass production line,
Corporate world of power and fierce control,
Sprawling global dream.

Do world gained but soul that's lost now seem
Words of foolishness,
Musings time has taught us to repress?
Knowing laws can't be one size fits all,
Most free-marketeers resent the state,
Let's return to what is ours and small
Find new visions we'd self-regulate,
Wiser dreams to dream?

15

China is the culprit many name,
Earth's new chimneystack
Darkening air with smut and carbon black,
Stoking world emissions by a third,
They've become the villains of the piece.
In shaming them all western shame is blurred,
Our condemning China's spewed increase
Hollow noise of blame.

When demanding others call a halt
Do we then forget
How most multinationals offset
Labour costs decamping anywhere
They can get their cheaper pound of flesh
And at will contaminate the air
In Korea, China, Bangladesh?
Who is not at fault?

Marketplace belief we now abjure
And begin to face
How industry and climate interlace,
Though for years we've kept them both at odds.
Nature claims the heed we must afford,
Will no longer tolerate false gods.
If economy and climate care accord
We may still endure.

16

Although righteously our west may rail
At how China's coal
Hikes the carbon count, we play our role
In abetting China's splurge. What now
Should a mooted change of course prove true?
Reaping sun and wind they'd show us how
Pioneers they'd lead the world anew,
Blaze a greener trail.

If the east were quicker now to cope
With our global threat
We would have to shift our blame mindset.
Think if east and west were to decide
To curtail pollution of earth's air—
Turning back from pending ecocide,
Though there's much may be beyond repair,
We could dare to hope.

No matter who's to blame what's done is done.
We who now have known
How a plague makes east and west its own,
Know we risk our being when we cause
Habitats to shift, how high the stakes
If we undo our nature's fragile gauze.
Blaming none for all our greed's mistakes
We atone as one.

17

Wantonly we've let our planet warm
Let its ice shelves thaw
So travelling storms that gather draw
Warm water's heat and rising steam,
Drive the wind's increase as rain-bombs burst,
Overwhelm with floods now so extreme
Whole urban swathes are submersed—
Disasters now our norm.

Yet we name our hurricanes like friends;
Once remembered by a year,
Now for some their names still instil fear:
Dorian, Katrina, Sandy, Jeanne,
Sally, Wilma, Rita, Floyd, Paulette,
Harvey, Teddy, Cristobal, Irene,
List we half-recall can't forget—
Who knows how this ends?

At this pace how will we still survive?
Decades worth of thaw
All at once as early greens foresaw.
Nature's deep time hurried and distressed;
Thawing icebergs crumple into seas,
Match the speed with which we are obsessed,
Feed new hurricanes' intensities—
World in overdrive.

18

For eons all earth's living things unfurled
In surroundings that
Shaped them best to suit a habitat;
Now we humans in our hardihood
For one second in earth's saga's span
While thinking everything is understood
At our risk discover how we can
Alter nature's world.

Hard to fathom how creation sifts
Millennia to find
How so many habitats combined
Weave a complex web of compromise.
Life adapts to what supports or wounds
In vast interplays of unseen ties
All sustained or finely reattuned—
Nature's subtle shifts.

In our power we humans were unique
Able to undo
Networks of rapport before we knew
Or had cared to know if humans ought
Not for short-term gain without a plan,
Let our mastery outpace our thought,
Doing what we can because we can,
Awed by our technique.

19

All the while we think we are in charge
Nature clips our wings;
Our relationship attaches strings—
Being one will bring us back to earth.
When we trust what's measured, all we gauge,
Calculating all for all we're worth,
Nature's eagle we can never cage
Still remains at large.

Insects we're determined to attack
With our poison sprays
Sometimes by adapting can amaze,
They mutate, flare back a thousand-fold;
Or their rival insects propagate,
So environments we try to mould
Uncurbed by insects killed retaliate,
Nature fighting back.

Trees and vegitation's debris fall—
Deep compressing plunge
Eons turn into a carbon sponge
Stowing toxins that burnt coal emits
While its carbon warms our atmosphere.
Humbled by each storm and cyclone blitz,
Let us let earth's debris rest, revere
Nature's longer haul.

20

Frozen eras trapped in Arctic ice
Still secrete disease
That our global warming may unfreeze
Reanimating prehistoric pests;
Our immunities will not then know
How such pathogens make their conquests.
In our greenhouse comforts we now throw
Deadly games of dice.

Yellow fever once the jungle dread
In the Amazon,
Mosquito-borne it has we know now gone
Far beyond rainforests, drawing near
Rio and São Paulo at the rate
Of some three miles every year.
Dangers of the jungle radiate—
Tropics northward spread.

In God's geotime eyeblinks ago
Though the Black Death spread
Leaving some three-fifths of Europe dead
It would travel at its victim's speed
Never further than its carrier could.
In our time no distances impede
Raging through our earth's one neighbourhood—
To our cost we know.

21

Much of our exhaust, seawaters soak,
Fossil fuels spew;
Near one-third of humans' CO_2
Feeds the brine that feasts an algae bloom
Leaving in our oceans vast dead zones—
Fish die in these waters' barren womb,
Deadly locker room of Davy Jones
Where our oceans choke.

Coral reefs those ecosystems grown
Where one-fourth of all
Fish at least make them a port of call
Die when bleaching warmer waters slay
Zooxanthellae their secure food fare
And a coral city's wiped away—
Source of food for us a sunken layer,
Ocean's twilight zone.

Hard to fathom the damage we can do
If we stop the slow
Circulation of deep ocean flow.
Gulf stream driven by its heat and salt
Moving north grows cold and dense and falls
Flowing south but think if through our fault
Europe freezes as this cycle stalls—
World as known askew.

22

Marvellous how still our lungs can cope
With polluted air
Filthy, nastier than we're aware.
Hotter still it grows the more ozone,
So our planet is one dirty bowl
Where we're swaddled in our comfort zone,
Our habitat's polluted glory hole
Earth's dust envelope.

Grey sun-blotted days when smog is rife
And oxygen is less
Smaller particle pollution's stress
Bears on how alert our brain can be;
Paint and petrol damage mental power,
Speed old age, impair a pregnancy.
Willy-nilly now we're living our
Kamikaze life.

Aerosols and sprays we have designed
Wreak their harm on all
Breathing in each dusty urban sprawl.
Yet non-carbon gas deflects sunlight,
Slows the warming down so we appease
Our concern about pollution's blight.
Clear skies or breathing-linked disease,
Our own double bind.

23

Decades now we've brushed it all aside
Turning our deaf ear
To advice we didn't want to hear.
Most species soon will yearly need to shift
Some one thousand metres not to die;
All the same we let the planet drift
Turning a blind eye we still deny
Our own ecocide.

Even if we open ears and eyes
And know each case and fact,
Measure tragedies and how to act,
Try to put all nature through the hoops
Thinking we still somehow stand outside,
Nature's tipping points and feedback loops
Can surprise, and curbing human pride
Cut us down to size.

Greed and soft convenience so enmesh
Our desires unless
Grief is ours. We easily can suppress
Any fear or fact as we consume.
Laws we need yet not just laws alone;
There's such hope our spirits still can room
If compassion takes our hearts of stone,
Gives us hearts of flesh.

24

Should we even now pull in our horns
Damage will be done—
Climate migrants seek a cooler sun,
Glaciers have shrunk and sheet ice breaks,
Cattle graze where once rainforest stood—
We will have to live with greed's mistakes.
All a world has lost is lost for good
History forewarns.

Northern male white rhinos are extinct—
Loss of habitat,
War and poaching of their horns bought at
Asian markets as some magic cure.
Scientists seed southern surrogates,
Hope to breed a male who will mature
For the females greed deprived of mates;
Nature half-hoodwinked.

Never too late to think how we behave.
Yes, for us who know
Plenty's horn there's much we may forego,
Luxuries, indulgences we'll miss
Yet will soon forget as love insists
We pull back from our self-made abyss,
Leave our aftercomers what exists,
All we still may save.

25

When Watt watched a kettle on the boil
Jenny spun her wheel;
Come electric power, come coal and steel
And our want to fabricate en masse,
Everything scaled up pursuing wealth.
We keep fracking oil, extracting gas,
We pollute and risk our own good health
On this earth we spoil.

We who saw the dirt and smut of coal
Watch another phase
As tech-wizards who at first amaze
Turning to new avarice will spy,
Auction off what was their moral sense—
From first promises so far a cry.
Once enough to earn at health's expense,
Greed wants mind and soul.

Such constant need for more than we require
So we still behave
As if living just for what we crave
And greed now seems to be our only aim.
World at risk as never seen before—
Will our generation take the blame?
Can we mortals ask ourselves once more
What do we desire?

Behind the Screen

1

When the serpent came and tempted Eve
Had she ever seen a spring come twice?
Did she along with Adam not believe

Even in creation's paradise
Seasons would return if they could trust
In what's patterned and yet not precise,

Freeing things to change and readjust,
Let sap improvise when each tree shed?
Instead they're overcome with lust

For control, predicting what's ahead,
They devour the apple, sure they'll see
Everything that their creator said

Only was so they'd not own the tree—
His omniscience his last defence.
Satan baited them with certainty

Would they not outdo God's opulence?
Knowledge is the fruit that might enthral,
Hold in check the riskful future tense.

Tragedy of that one apple's fall,
Our first garden's greed to know it all.

2

Click or tap. All knowledge now accessed—
Gone the tracking down, the search ordeal,
Lost all serendipities of quest.

Though we longed for things, yet once we'd feel
Half of our delight was in the wait,
Sure that some mirage would yet be real.

We required delay so we'd gestate
Longings deep enough for time to fill,
Yearned for what we could anticipate.

Even in our thirst for life we'd still
Fallen under our desire's own spell—
Joy deferred, a slower pending thrill.

We no longer trust all will be well—
Time is money now and waits for none,
Time is not the time that used to tell.

No delights postponed or no long run—
What we want now everybody deems
Better all at once than one by one.

Slacked by our computers' instant streams,
Each desire quenched at the speed of dreams.

3

Googol, still a playful guileless word—
For nine and ninety zeros after ten—
Could for any keen computer nerd

Conjure quantities beyond our ken,
Myriads of nets which interweave
And new skills to comb them where and when

We are moved to search or to retrieve
Data, algorithms that they've designed
Bringing us at once the knowledge we've

Often needed weeks to try to find.
Whiz-kids interlink and organise
Hives of information they've streamlined.

Flair and genius will at first give rise
To fresh dreams of knowledge for us all,
Vast new worlds that take us by surprise.

Virtuous still before temptation's fall,
Computer students form their partnerships,
Gather all that's known from webs they crawl.

Silicon's own valley's memory chips,
Netted knowledge at our fingertips.

4

Even if outstanding nonetheless
Rage for finespun measurement decrees
Mentions rank a scholar's work success.

Two young geeks combine their expertise,
Reckon counts of website links will too
Find a precedence that guarantees

Searches ordered in a way that's new;
Smarter than just searching by key phrase,
They'll provide for us our overview.

First in student dorms those youthful days,
Then a friend's garage but growing fast,
All will move into another phase.

Doctorates now ditched, their lives recast,
Rich investors offer to bankroll
More; their search engine unsurpassed

They'll by supervotes still keep control
While offering initial public shares,
Pledging they would never lose their soul.

'Don't be evil', their submission dares—
This will be a company that cares.

5

Virtuosos, super-prodigies,
Two professors' sons whose lives prepare
Both to navigate software with ease.

Surely such a pair were well-aware
How young countries crave a knowledge base,
Lack of information is unfair?

They're obsessed with haste as they outrace
All and driven by some inner need
Send their data into cyberspace.

Just the pace at which these two succeed—
Such intense excitement, even pride,
Everything they dreamed of up to speed.

Think of how search engines could provide
Reservoirs with all things up to date,
There for every one of us worldwide.

Here's a fairer world that they create—
Democratic knowledge seems so just,
Biased history's fast counterweight.

Such velocity leaves us nonplussed.
In all innocence we've learned to trust.

6

Upright founders scorned advertising—
Service to their users their ideal—
Then the sudden dot com world downswing.

'Surely I'm a schmuck or what's the deal?'
Asks one genius. So were they to be
One more start-up crushed by fortune's wheel?

Venture capital had left them free
To refine the earth's best search machine,
Earning fees from every licensee.

Now the bubble burst, though they had been
Sure they could succeed while ethical,
Their financiers begin to lean

On these wonder boys of principle.
There's a bottom line and balance sheet,
How much earned here on their capital?

Backers now are turning up the heat—
Such impatient money needs gain soon,
Venturers will threaten their retreat.

Must this dim their vision's honeymoon,
Devil-supping with too short a spoon?

7

Who had searched and when and where and what
Stored half-wittingly to help all find
Just exactly what they sought and not

To derive income—but now behind
Users' backs much knowledge once dismissed
Will become a rich resource that's mined.

All, they tell their users, to assist
Sending relevant advertisements.
Records of behaviour that exist,

What had been just surplus now presents
Ways to sidestep searching by keyword,
So instead they now to all intents

Misappropriate what is transferred
From the service of the user to
Target customers as undeterred

They keep thieving knowledge they accrue.
Their whole business starts to readjust,
Sell their searchers' private residue.

However justified, a breach of trust—
Once high-mindedness now money lust.

8

What we search do others have to know?
Yet so silently they had begun
To extract this information so

They can sell it on, although it's spun
As designed for users. They are paid
Not for every time that everyone

Gets their ads but just when they persuade
Searchers to then click through to their site.
How were we so easily betrayed?

Was the internet too recondite?
Lured by our convenience, unaware,
We only understand it in hindsight.

Times were ripe for ruthless laissez-faire,
Neo-cons command the marketplace;
Avarice was flaring everywhere.

Nine-eleven meant in cyberspace
Fear of terrorist tenacity
Licensed all surveillance just in case.

Parallel to dark audacity,
History had graced rapacity.

9

Privacy our right not to disclose
What we think, believe and own or do—
Best not known just how surveillance knows.

Nothing gives their searchers any clue—
Only backstage maestros are let know,
Covert priesthood, hidden inner few

All bound to secrecy and lying low
Lest they're found out at this snooping game
Or that anybody stop the flow

Of the data that they sell or claim
They had breached the trust they'd promised first.
Maybe rivals who now do the same

Might discover ruses they'd rehearsed
Since turning their still-trusting clientele
Into market products or at worst

Overtake their search machine and sell
More by stealth. The founders are obsessed
With concealment, driven to excel.

Mandarins who craving to contest,
Need to win where winning softly's best.

10

Dizzied by the net's velocity,
Here's the world we're told to take or leave,
How things are and how they have to be.

Any doubts about how they deceive
Serving us in name as they self-serve,
Any questioning the way they thieve

Or talk of how they maybe should observe
Rights of privacy and we soon find
They respond by touching our raw nerve.

Insecure, afraid of being behind,
We are told how we should understand
That technology too has a mind

All of its own which evolution planned—
Just as we had busted and had boomed
Guided by the market's unseen hand,

We must now be glad how we are doomed
To acquiesce in crawls that data scrape,
Our compliance with it all assumed.

What if we should press control-escape—
Cyberspace is surely ours to shape?

11

More that's earned, the more a lust dictates—
Newer snoop techniques to guarantee
Advertisers higher click-through rates.

Data bought lets marketers foresee
Who is likeliest to want to buy,
Targeted campaigns their golden key.

Most of us unmindful how they spy
On the face of things must bless the net.
Think of all the ways that we rely

On the speed of links or how we're let
Talk across the world to friends on screens,
See the children children now beget,

Or in pandemic days or quarantines
Zooms of company for which we yearned,
Half-aware of how behind the scenes

Dream's about-face since the business turned
Ruthless when the dot com bubble burst
Rides still roughshod to those trillions earned.

Double-faced this net is blessed and cursed;
The corruption of the best is worst.

12

Advertisers want to raise the bar—
Better targeting means to conceive
Bolder schemes to burgle who we are.

Spying more without a by your leave
In the guise of serving what we need,
New conveniences so they deceive,

Lulling us with ease till they succeed,
Waiting out incensed protesters who
Under laws too old can't curb their greed.

Shamed, they promise what they cannot do;
Self-reform would be to fail to know
All that best predicts an ad's click-through.

If they're cornered they may make a show
Of renaming schemes, admitting flaws,
Sending contracts where we must forego

Rights, agreeing to some click-wrap clause.
So it's grab and keep and let time flout
Norms of privacy, outdated laws.

Our convenience in turn dulls doubt;
Booty seekers swerve and ride it out.

13

Surplus information satisfied,
Numbers, patterns of our clicks, dwell times—
Now the hunt has moved to worlds outside.

Matching how the admen's ante climbs,
They're determined they will chart all space,
Reality the virtual now mimes.

Marvellous to call up any place,
Any street or house forgetting that
Street View cars had sent their database

Passwords, emails, transcripts of each chat,
Data they had pillaged from our screens,
While they colonised our habitat.

Not enough to trace our search machines,
They now poach our lives whole and entire—
Certainty is craved by any means.

Marketers must get what they require,
Surety enough to undergird
How they best control and steer desire.

Mappers of our lives they undeterred
Coax or shame, cajoling nudge and herd.

14

So deep the need in us to home, to roost
Somewhere where our secrets are our own—
Yet so easily we've been seduced.

Although exteriors at first were known,
Back-pack cameras nabbed all inside—
Nothing private, nothing left alone,

Surveillance leaves us nowhere we can hide.
In our overburdened lifestyles we've
Fallen prey to voices that provide

Answers to requests that can relieve
Us of tasks, our soothing maids of ease
Who follow our commands although they thieve.

Locks or light or thermostats but she's
Sniffing words like 'love', 'dislike' or 'bought',
Spying all the while she seems to please.

As smart listeners learn to read each thought,
Captives of our age's ease syndrome,
In our craving comfort we are caught.

Where is our shell? What sanctum won't they comb?
What or where can we now call our home?

15

Knowledge still the power it's always been—
Yet there's more than ever known before
In the offstage hands that snoop unseen.

We unwittingly till now forbore
Hindering their information flow,
Tapped by scams we're learning to abhor.

Chosen few alone who're in the know,
All the while pretending to inform,
Now create a world they claim to show.

Helpless in the face of this new norm,
Watched by eyes both near us and remote,
Nerdish billionaires take us by storm.

Our attitudes and traits, they've taken note—
Nothing's from their peeping eye exempt,
Selling goods or steering how we vote.

Knowledge is the fruit and serpents tempt—
Take the apple from the tree and eat!
Errancy control will soon pre-empt.

Power's unfair division by deceit,
Foisted by technology's elite.

16

Yes, to order knowledge once their goal—
Better now design society,
Shaping our existence as a whole.

No caprice of force or tyranny,
Just behaviour trained as they see best,
Smoothing out safe routes to certainty.

Eons and how far have we progressed?
If we were conditioned to behave,
So that when our lives had coalesced,

Programmed happiness could then enslave
Us to eons of the same song sung,
Note for note adhering to one stave.

No dissent or compromises wrung,
Unison, a tune no need to score,
No dissonance and no surprises sprung.

Certainty still Eden's apple's core—
Missioners of ease may seem benign
Selling sameness that they name rapport.

Those who know dictating by design—
All things solved when all fall into line.

17

So instinctively they've sussed us out,
Maestros of this age's own zeitgeist
Playing on our angst or on our doubt.

Freed from staider times we sacrificed
Old stabilities of sure lifestyles.
Gambling on new openness we've diced

On a bigger game, become exiles
From the lands of our own well-worn past,
Found our way by choice, by chance or trials.

Solo thrill of each iconoclast
Can so easily in time fall flat,
Feeling we have somehow been outcast.

Sensing this the clever technocrat,
Touting what is named connectedness,
Plunders when online we tweet and chat,

Feeds relentless hunger to express
Now our two-edged newfound liberty,
How in our freedom we know loneliness.

We still crave support though we are free,
Telling us we're who we're meant to be.

18

Not enough to watch us one by one—
Better know how we all interact—
Individual free will is overdone.

Since our social synergies are tracked,
Given this all-seeing God's eye view,
Independent wills have no impact.

You don't make a hive, a hive makes you.
Best you're trained to serve the honeycomb,
Never be among the errant few.

Computer gurus know that our genome
Steers how when alone we're incomplete,
Drawn by peers instinctively we home.

What others do we're pressured to repeat.
Millennia had taught us what is just,
Yet the wisdom time and lives accrete

Now outdated, told we must adjust,
Does society become a swarm,
Certainty supplant our human trust?

Any well-run hive demands a norm,
Fellow feelings worked till we conform.

19

What is this need to post our latest news,
Telling all to those the web calls friends?
So, so many we reach. How many views?

Nothing very much, just odds and ends
Claiming our few moments in the sun,
Warmth on which our self-esteem depends.

Harmless habit nervously begun,
We're drawn daily in and soon obsessed,
Waiting on a comment when there's none.

What is billed as contact turns at best
Loneness to a kind of ratings race
As in cyberspace desires contest.

Though we count each virtual embrace,
Something still is empty at the core,
Solitudes have failed to interface.

Vicious circles turning then once more,
We, for all we know how we despaired,
Gambling, post again and hope we score.

Craving peer assent all are ensnared;
Self-worth measured by what's liked and shared.

20

Granting us a life that rebegins,
Once we thought a pardon could wipe clean,
All might be forgiven, all our sins.

Ruthlessly in cyberspace they glean
Any breach or blunder that can taunt
Us and keep our misdeeds evergreen.

Norms that youth's exuberance will flaunt,
Images unwisely some may post,
Every indiscretion comes to haunt.

Searches place all scandals uppermost,
Rubbing in whatever mistakes made,
So our pasts remain a tethered ghost.

While in secret privacy's betrayed,
Openly available on sites,
Credit ratings, debts, the fines we've paid.

Nothing is absolved, all stored in bytes;
No clean slate, no chance of amnesty,
No infringement mercy underwrites.

Each transgression there for all to see;
Damned to internet eternity.

21

World in vain we tried to dominate
Brings us in our weakness back to earth.
Taught how living things reciprocate,

Surely short-term gains were never worth
All the damage selfishness has wrought,
New migrations, pathogens and dearth.

Finally we've learned our globe is fraught
With uncertainty and know how fast
Eons of this life could come to nought.

Now an avarice which by contrast
With abuses known had seemed benign;
Netting us a priesthood has amassed

All they need to know to undermine
Who we are, to shape desires, entice
Us until we are who they design.

New smart phone, smart watch, each smart device
Tracking us in our mundanity,
Dooming us to our fool's paradise.

Earth we've risked in our own vanity,
Greed subverts our frail humanity.

22

All the blogospheres and Twitter news,
Online life more real than our lived lives—
Like the ink that paper can't refuse,

Tweets, chat slang or memes, whatever thrives
Feeding information true or fake;
Any hosting platform just connives

Even when democracy's at stake.
Ideologues post messages of hate,
Falsehoods spread for slander's wanton sake,

Stories that they choose to circulate
Where they mix a grain of truth with lies,
So conspire to undermine a state.

Platforms with their bots or cookie spies,
Feigning care when somehow they're found out,
Make new promises, apologise—

Promises we know they soon will flout.
Smudges of untruth, a world askew,
Everything we see we now must doubt.

Boundaries so blurred—what's false? what's true?
Will we ever dare to trust anew?

23

Genius of an age, the brightest youths—
Some who would inform the world for free—
Turn now billionaire computer sleuths.

Kings of internet who once might be
Menders of our earth's so many ills.
Think if they had spent their energy

Or used their minds, their hearts, their wills
Understanding problems we all face,
Think if they had brought to bear their skills

Puzzling how might leaders set the pace
In reducing how we all pollute,
How they'd save our soon endangered race.

Or might they have helped the destitute
Even tried to succour those in pain?
Instead like Eve they steal forbidden fruit.

Gifted, masterminds of thought and brain
Middle-age in their own greed's black hole.
Cyberspace's kings are slaves to gain

In the counting houses they control,
Counting out the price paid for a soul.

24

As the deaths from our pandemic mount,
States in order to curtail its spread
Struggle, somehow trying to keep count

Of each citizen and keep ahead,
So should they fall prey to this disease
All their contacts will be known instead

Of discovering by slow degrees
Who the stricken had been with or met.
Tracing all on mobiles guarantees

That at least such tracking on the net,
Curbs a spread. We have no time for doubts.
Thankful for such apps we can forget

Knowing at all times our whereabouts
Brings its risks and we may fail to see
All the sacred privacies it flouts.

Should regimes and net tycoons agree,
State control and avarice align,
Where this leads no one can now foresee.

Tracking to protect us once benign,
Easily in time might turn malign.

25

Internet surveillance now so rife,
If not soon curtailed by laws and rights
Such unseen control will usurp life.

Only by policing use of sites
Are we sure that we are not betrayed—
Even then with endless legal fights—

Just as once all factories were made
Work more human hours and to ensure
Labourers in turn were better paid.

Yet if life's full richness should endure,
Trusting to uncertainty's caress,
Generosity must be our cure.

Stretching hearts beyond rapaciousness,
We desire a paradigm re-shift
Where to own is not to dispossess.

Ours the stewardship of this earth's gift
In some greater whole we learn to heed,
Mixing sweet excess with sweeter thrift.

Laws may curb the idols of our greed—
Visions of abundance still our need.

Desiring

1

Pathogens have brought us to our knees—
Thirty thousand times more miniscule
Than one grain of salt, a new disease
Following no pattern or known rule,
Sneaking symptomless can quickly fool
Pride and show in nature's filigree
How we're frail in our humanity.

There'll be at least a million worldwide gone—
From their shades their silences implore,
Begging us as life starts moving on
Not to try returning or restore
All exactly as it was before.
Will this outbreak be a watershed?
Can we hear the cries of Covid's dead?

Skewed, bled dry by our short-term excess,
Mother Earth's depleted by our greed.
How will we relearn our creatureness?
Checking, scrolling, read by ads we read,
Wants arise we're shaped to think we need.
In the dust of all that we acquire,
What in our frail world do we desire?

2

What is worth the sum of our desire
And deserves all strength, all mind, all thought?
Where's the source of meaning to inspire
Longings for what can't be sold or bought?
Surely human hearts have always sought
Somehow to make sense of why we are
Flickering here between a quark and star.

Months and months all lives were quarantined—
Sabbath from the hectic carousel—
Restless half-unwittingly we're weaned
From the constant drive to buy or sell,
Forced retreat for some that broke the spell
Opening up the marvel of new days,
Freeing time for wonder and for praise.

Sunrise, nightfall less bothered by the clock,
Rhythms of our creation reappear.
Crisis is a time for taking stock
How on earth both joy and grief cohere,
Glorify a source both far and near.
Breath of life beyond and yet within—
God in his eternity breaks in.

3

All eternity is round and slow—
Trees inscribe each year a grateful ring;
Days by nights by days' adagio
Number moons in months that turn each spring
Into summers so each fall can bring
Winters yielding to spring suns that climb
In the fullness of unfolding time.

Ungrounded in our seasons all is speed
Measured out in minutes hastening by;
Time is money seconds count in greed.
Ever-pinging mobile phones' third eye
Watches us as urged we click and buy.
Saving what we never have to spare,
Velocity consumes our time and care.

Eons we forget deep in our bones
Borrowed from the stars our carbon dust—
Yet such damage our small age condones
And so much destroyed left us in trust.
Can we still escape greed's boom and bust,
In the deeper time of prayer regrow?
All eternity is round and slow.

4

Evolution's every change was slow
Sorting out the fittest who'd survive
And adapting best went with the flow
Of contingency and so would thrive.
One family tree of genes till we arrive
And here we are all legatees of theirs—
Will we prove to be ungrateful heirs?

Who'd return to grinding poverty
Or forego a longer life in health?
But our planet's now in jeopardy—
One percent owns over half the wealth—
This rapacity destroys by stealth
And who knows where such avarice will lead.
Will we learn to curb outrageous greed?

Linking forebears with those still to come,
Just as we remember we prepare
Thriving is no zero sum.
Stewards of God's sacred earth we care
For our children's children; seeds we bear
Dream what yet will grow, a future planned—
Trees live longer than the planting hand.

5

Handing on this life is our success—
Countless generations down the line
We can be the forebears they will bless
For our seeing nature's own design,
Where in habitats all lives combine,
Bound in the abundance of it all,
One creation for the longer haul.

Always in advancement's hungry name
Each year we've taken twice the earth can bear.
All the biosphere for us fair game,
Fouling our own nest and half-aware,
We espouse an easy laissez-faire;
Endless quests for progress can't stand still,
Empty more than nature can refill.

Enough, enough to be just thankful for
This our world so whole and so entire
In its balanced state of self-rapport.
God of love, God in the bush's fire
Hides a face in all we most desire—
Life and light creation's golden bough,
Our own holy land is here and now.

6

Hurtling towards the moon before they'd land
That first crew had snapped the earth behind;
Frail and wisped it almost looked unmanned,
Each blotched surface vague and ill defined
As the moon had seemed to humankind—
Mystifying disk, a wraithlike face,
Waxing, waning stepping stone to space.

Would a flag then claim the rocky moon?
Surely when we saw the image sent
In our hearts we must have known that soon
We'd admit for all of our dissent,
All of our variety, we're meant
In our Milky Way's own spiral arm
To protect our fragile globe from harm.

Is the deepest greed a lust for power,
Fame and wealth a means to gain control,
Playing God to build a Babel's tower
With one view, one lore, one tongue, one goal?
Where's love's vision that could make us whole,
Dream a world where no one's overrun.
Glorious we babble yet are one.

7

Progress still our one and only dream—
Though we know all cultures rise and fall,
Somehow we believe we'll reign supreme;
Driven by a market's free-for-all,
We can't see how nature starts to stall.
Empires die of their excessive needs—
Are we biting now the hand that feeds?

Is a slow and piecemeal change enough?
Many who despair of politics
Claim that we will need regimes who're tough
Or demand we find a technofix,
Problems engineered by our skilled tricks.
Cures utopian and those too small—
Maybe best combine the work of all.

More than anything a humbler heart—
Paradigms must shift our old mindset,
Shape the jazz of life lived à la carte:
Cana's wine or jubilee's wiped debt,
Misdeeds we have permission to forget,
Give and take God's lavish earth requires
Home again in generous desires.

8

Nature is our home and habitat—
Yet so long a backdrop and resource
That at will each clever technocrat
Simply as a matter of due course
Could dominate or master it by force;
By our needs all beings are defined,
Channelled to the wants of humankind.

Trying to control by power and wealth
Dominance must be a kind of fear;
Scared of futures catching us by stealth,
We can't see the glory that is here—
Since we do not trust we have to steer.
Never enough as even in excess
Still we dread our own precariousness.

God of our surprises tell us how
Not to master or control, instead
Let all interwoven being wow
Us with hybrid beauty you've crossbred.
Let us look around not look ahead!
Now is where our past and future chime
Deep in your polyphony of time.

9

Time and time again we'll think we know
Who we are, who we'll become for good.
Surely there's no other way to go,
Any further shifts are best withstood
Now we've found our own pure personhood?
Then in fresh encounters we succumb
To that someone we must yet become.

Who we are is not in our control—
All adulterated, never pure,
In contingency another role.
Constantly recast we best endure
Swayed by some new mutual allure.
In such shared infectiousness we thrive,
Changing for each other we're alive.

Was it all a dream, the choice, the chance
When unlikely matches had begun
In a serendipitous romance
And each sense of self could seem undone,
As two utter strangers fused as one
In contamination's push and shove,
Trusting to a God's contagious love?

10

Trust comes from a root that once meant firm,
Solid, staunch and steadfast as a tree,
Whose shared root implies the longer term;
So no wonder standing firm that we
Breathe with trees in mutuality—
Oxygen we need they can re-give.
In each other's shade our beings live.

Boulders in their roots a flood can't budge
Trees reach up for sunlight to feed leaves
While their soil is worked by worms that drudge;
Sunned or underfoot all breathes and heaves
In concerted webs a forest weaves
From assemblages of throbbing life—
Worlds so ravenous, so rich, so rife.

Every being's story intertwines,
Breathing in each other's breathed waste
Ours are unintentional designs;
Though at first so much can seem displaced
All once more is somehow interlaced,
In their brokenness lives readjust—
Our desire to live relearns to trust.

11

Each environment relearns to cope
With what change disturbances invite,
Readapting wildlife's envelope:
Forest trees that fall leave gaps for light,
In their wake room for the sun's delight;
Floods and fires can alter a terrain
Nature's household will reform again.

In our fear we dream a perfect past—
All before disturbance was serene—
Though through change we never could forecast
We become what never might have been.
Can we trust, embrace the unforeseen?
God who threw our evolution's dice
Holds in store a startling paradise.

Undisturbed how would our heaven be?
Surely our creator will create
Realms of joy. Though tribulation-free,
God's love less one kingdom's steady state
More a flow we'll travel in full spate,
Glory multiplying glory's sum,
Kingdom after kingdom yet to come.

12

Like stray spores that come what may must fly
Thoughts about the One who's worth desire
Over time both float and amplify;
It seems as though our seekings never tire,
After centuries we still inquire
What could be the mind of such a One
Who though sought is fathomed yet by none.

We who still through time have always sought,
Being caught up in our own routine,
Lack the span to focus on such thought—
Our attention somewhere in-between,
We are scrolling down our laptop screen,
Dulled by acquisition, profit's drive,
Yet desire for meaning and to thrive.

Still the swirling spores of thought will drift
Through imagination's stratosphere
Trying to understand the One whose gift
Is this life's own sweet abundance here,
Source to which our innerness will veer,
Circling, whirling, close and far again,
One who's near and still beyond our ken.

13

Maybe we've been near and did not know
How we had not seen a sacred spoor;
Self-absorbed we'd missed the afterglow,
Faintest glance, a glimmer now obscure
Vestige of a shine which means for sure
That a silent glory passed unseen
Leaving intimations of a sheen.

How to be alert, to snatch a glance,
Catch a solitary stolen peek,
Glimpse the back if not the countenance?
Even if absconding or oblique,
Yet it must be everything we seek
Though we only barely comprehend
Our desire's beginning and its end.

Maybe touching someone's loving hand,
Laughter shared with friends on sunlit days,
Lavish gifts our hearts half-understand
Or perhaps unbidden words of praise
In a passing stranger's sideways gaze—
Footprint of a presence, trail or trace;
God of hints and signs, a hidden face.

14

Hard to face not being in control
Shaped by the Enlightenment we're sure
Part by part we'll apprehend the whole
And that nothing will remain obscure.
Know-all visions we must now abjure—
Part and parcel of what we observe,
Nature still has secrets to preserve.

We have no privileged bird's-eye overview
Comprehending everything below
As we learn what once perhaps we knew—
Sweeter lowliness of letting go,
Knowing there are things we'll never know.
In this world we are both in and of,
Much we only understand in love.

In the midst of what we can't control,
When the dreams of our perfection lapse,
Losing sight of what had seemed our goal,
Can it be that there are rifts and gaps,
Some interstices in our mishaps,
Where we creep again before we crawl,
Muddling nearer to the All in All?

15

What is all this craving for success,
Endless need to score a better score?
Some fresh sign of status to possess,
Some new golden calf we can adore?
Wanting always more and more and more,
Up and up we climb the greasy pole—
Trying to gain a world we lose a soul.

Something insecure in us still drives
Such pursuit of power and fame and wealth,
Using up the sum of our quick lives.
Maybe thinking riches might buy health
Come night's thief that catches all by stealth,
Some see wielding power as self-defence,
So surround themselves with opulence.

Is there one outstanding moment when
We find a peace in simply knowing how
There's no need to find desires again?
All our being wants us to avow
One desire so full that there is now
Nothing needed over and above
Letting fame and fortune be to love.

16

Love—a word we're quick to throw about—
Yet for all confusions, each false start
Or mistake, some hope in us can't doubt,
Even if the wounds of loss still smart
We are searching for a counter-heart
Where our core, our innermost desire,
Dares again to walk love's highest wire.

In so many narratives we catch
Longing deeply woven in a plot
We in our own listening hearts can match.
So we find we want no matter what
That two fall in love and tie the knot.
We espouse a story's twist and turn,
Hope for what two characters both yearn.

Does it all just happen in a dream
Where each lover's life is one sweet sleep,
So that in each other's arms they seem
Loving up love's promises they keep
To still deepen what they'd once thought deep.
In each warm embrace God's swift caress;
Being loved our greatest happiness.

17

Autumn being the time the sap won't flow,
We might think each broadleaf tree then grieves;
Yet how slowly, patiently they show
Crimson and banana-yellow leaves,
Even though all know how fast wind thieves
Every branch's glory in one squall—
Leaves that fall are loveliest of all.

How our green ambitions ramify,
Years of our expanding rings ahead,
Sap in spate our limit is the sky.
Why should we then ever think we'd shed
Leafage once so full-veined and sun-fed,
Ask to what when bare we would aspire,
How the seasons would refine desire?

One another's countersignature,
Autumn hues fulfil the dreams of springs;
All a season burgeoned, now mature,
Praises turning beauty in all things.
In our heartwood's concentrated rings
One desire our lifetimes now distil,
Slowly to succumb to God's ripe will.

18

Will our globe succumb to selfishness
Idolising Aaron's golden calf?
Under pressure so much talk of stress—
Are we all too greedy now by half,
So forgetting how to play, to laugh;
Worlds of deals where we want quid pro quo
Lack the giddy freedom to let go.

Yet how much can any of us own?
Many have enough and more but still
Insecurities no goods atone;
Need for more a black hole we can't fill,
Nothing now acquired can fill the bill.
Some now dizzy with excess and power
Hoard belongings in their gated tower.

In our busyness are we aware
These swift lives of ours with which we toy
Scurry by? It seems we hardly care
What desires frivolities destroy.
Has our greed forgotten Eden's joy?
Foolishness of so much fun postponed—
God of love's delight we have disowned.

19

Delighting in creation as its guest,
Our desire no longer is control—
Prayer is mostly gratitude expressed.
Even thanking with both heart and soul,
What can we still add to what is whole?
Though acclaim may seem superfluous,
Praising such a fullness fulfils us.

Thankfulness still keeps the past in mind,
Layers what is with all that was before;
We both look ahead and look behind,
So we sometimes find we must implore,
In the light of what we have ask more.
Though not in control we still must hope,
Even beg for things we need to cope.

We cry out and trust no cry's in vain
As we slowly come to realise,
Though we seek so often we attain
Not what's sought but taken by surprise
Get all asked for in another guise.
With our God in turn we too conspire,
Pray to know what best we should desire.

20

Maybe we are praying to be wise,
To discern how over the long run
We can flourish and yet realise
That we best pass on what we've begun
By imparting practices from one
Generation to the next so they
Make what's ours their own for their own day.

Heavens we desire we too create,
Patterns of behaviour to sustain,
How in turn to steer a ship of state;
Though aware it never can attain
Full perfection, we will try again,
Mending where we blunder, where we slip,
Wise and constant in our stewardship.

So let peace be what we have begun,
World now turning over a new leaf—
We who walk here under heaven's sun,
Whether in belief or non-belief,
Solidarity our leitmotiv.
Part of God's creation we create;
Our desire we too must incarnate.

21

Even though we're loved we too are called
To embrace what best we know we do;
So desire by which we are enthralled
Shows us all its richness and breaks through
To display a heaven tried and true
Where persistence keeps revealing how
We create our heaven here and now.

Desire for us is neither whim nor mood—
Beckoned we all know we must obey.
Work becomes an act of gratitude,
Faithfulness from day to day to day
Somehow almost merging toil and play.
Ours a calling nothing else can mute,
One long-term desire, a life's pursuit.

None of us believes we work alone,
When we best achieve we self-transcend—
What would we succeed in on our own?
We fulfil each other; to one end
Our overlappings that both clash and blend,
Callings interwoven in one choir
Round a cantus firmus of desire.

22

Tragedy reorients desire—
One coronavirus spanned our globe,
Busily it knew it must acquire
Hosts so it survived and while each microbe
Is a cell, a virus has to probe
Changes in the guesting berth it needs;
So at our expense a virus breeds.

In a fog of habit walking blind
There's no reason to reorient.
All our fond routines once undermined,
Many shaken to their fundament
Wonder what to date their lives have meant.
Softly in each day's own pleasant mire,
Had we half-forgotten real desire?

Tumult is a time for taking stock.
What is all our avarice now worth?—
Some are asking of themselves in shock.
One's excess becomes another's dearth;
Can't we be wise gardeners of God's earth?
Life undone by lives beyond our need,
Earth in turmoil punishes our greed.

23

Greed demands search engines always pry,
Algorithms snoop on us unseen;
Barons of the net's all-ogling eye
Catching what we search and do on screen.
They'll sell on details their spywares glean
Stoking up each whim and fake desire—
Marketeers soon have our souls on hire.

Comfort first no matter what's at stake,
Touching 'I accept' without a thought,
We will find we do what it may take
To obtain some item we have sought
Sent to us the moment it is bought.
Wanting what we want without delay,
All our small desires one click away.

Is convenience our besetting sin,
Need for ease with which we are imbued?
How did self-enslavement then begin?
In our own destruction we collude,
Gratifying every whim and mood;
In each plush amenity we bask,
What things matter we forget to ask.

24

What on earth now matters most of all,
What is worth the sum of striving hearts?
We who bear the flaws of Adam's fall,
Even as we play our walk-on parts,
Know advances come in fits and starts;
All imperfect, never quite entire,
Yet a world that's shaped by our desire.

Sores of centuries still haunt us now,
Worlds of us and them where power-obsessed
In our long unhearing we allow
Others' different cries to be suppressed
As in greed we foul the global nest.
Poor and broken we have left behind;
History lists the blindfolds of our mind.

One in joy and in adversity,
Difference embraced not just allowed
We can love a world's diversity.
Past missteps now openly avowed,
Our desire a world of which we're proud;
Poised between our thanks and hope's rebirth—
As in heaven so we dream on earth.

25

Our dream is drawn far further than we yearn.
Dazzled more than we could ever hope,
Our desire outpaced at every turn—
With such lavishness we barely cope;
Awed by boundless height and depth and scope,
In our longing we can never tire,
So desirable what we desire.

Maker and creation not discrete,
Earth and heaven somehow intertwined—
If inspired God's want and ours both meet.
Such desire and ours once they're aligned
Grant us insights to that copious mind;
So each day creation rebegun,
All desire and will converge in one.

Anywhere out of a heaven's blue
When besotted by joy's radiance,
All the world is new, forever new.
Glory glimpsed in one astounding glance,
Love's freelancing we have caught by chance;
Taken by surprise we double take—
We desire our God for God's own sake.

Epilogue

Where to now? We know we can't return
To old greeds that play with nature's fire—
Never such an urgent need to learn
How to shape our world with new desire.

Science, arts or purse and politics
History and hope quintets express,
Yet this mesh of faults we need to fix—
Vision is best tested under stress.

Though new desire may drive new human care,
Yet we work to find the way and will,
Moves to hasten overdue repair—
We must be creation's menders still.

No long-fingered decades now to waste
In our world so one and interlaced.

(ii)

So easily we might self-second-guess
In such urgency begin to doubt
How our craft can tend a globe's distress,
Wonder if all art is opting out.

Just to praise creation's strands' one weave,
To reshape desire is still to act;
Seers of the whole our task to leave
Earth as is in heaven's prayer intact.

We too serve whose calling is to plumb
Glories of a world seen in the round.
Trailers and foretaste of kingdom come
Show in shape and hue, in word and sound.

Seeing how all things connect we trace
The eternal in each now our lives embrace.

(iii)

Every choice we make plays dominoes;
Globe-wide no economy's discrete,
Cyber world both drives our greed and shows
Others how as profligates we cheat.

Soon eight billion earth can still sustain
If we curb conveniences we crave
And as brothers' keepers unlike Cain,
Avoid excess, rethink how we behave.

New practices and things we must forego,
As some in luxury will strive to find
Bigger hearts so we do not now sow
Vengeance's seeds in those we'd leave behind

Love's creation tends our human needs,
When one world reins in its wants and greeds.

(iv)

For so long geography mandates
Lebensraum defence, power's bag of tricks—
Will we grow beyond our nation states,
Us and them of geopolitics?

Cities home two-thirds of humankind—
In these hubs of opulence or dearth
All our loyalties so intertwined
Ask if we can still repair our earth.

Pollution and all pests ignore frontiers,
We've no boundaries to guard or fix,

Humanity now thrives or disappears;
Healing planet-wounds our politics.

No captives of a chance geography—
World of neither us nor them but we.

(v)

Once we know there's no unknowingness,
Much we could but know we must not do;
Blessings yet temptations to transgress
Apple bitten we may come to rue.

All the marvels sciences can seize,
Magic bullets, nature's wonder's cache,
Vaccinations warding off disease—
Yet one fission turns our globe to ash.

Techno-dreams of internettedness,
Surprise of talking face to face on screen,
Worlds of knowledge, free for all access,
Gifts the snooping maestros will demean.

Always what we should not, what we should;
What we know now we must know for good.

(vi)

In a reckless world which greeds destroy
How we shape desire now make or break—
Will we trust fulfilment in God's joy,
All creation loved for love's own sake?

Joy that is before and after time
Is already here and now if we
In our desire can shift greed's paradigm—
So the love with which you have loved me

May now be in them and I in them.
Millennia in turn will pass and still
From this farewell prayer all futures stem,
Every choice we make for good or ill.

Trust in how both heaven and earth conspire
Glories in one ultimate desire.